ROBERT E. LEE

Troll Associates

ROBERT E. LEE

by Keith Brandt

Illustrated by John Lawn

Troll Associates

Library of Congress Cataloging in Publication Data

Brandt, Keith, (date)
    Robert E. Lee.

    Summary: A brief biography of the engineer, Confeder-
ate general, and college president, remembered as an
excellent military leader and a great American.
    1. Lee, Robert E. (Robert Edward), 1807-1870—Juvenile
literature.   2. Generals—United States—Biography—
Juvenile literature.   3. Confederate States of America.
Army—Biography—Juvenile literature. [1. Lee, Robert E.
(Robert Edward), 1807-1870. 2. Generals. 3. Confederate
States of America. Army—Biography.   4. United States—
History—Civil War, 1861-1865—Biography] I. Lawn,
John, ill. II. Title.
E467.1.L4B784   1985   973.7'3'0924 [92]   84-2687
ISBN 0-8167-0278-0 (lib. bdg.)
ISBN 0-8167-0279-9 (pbk.)

One of the most highly respected men in American history served as a Confederate general during the Civil War. He was an excellent military leader, and Northerners and Southerners alike share the feeling that Robert E. Lee was a great American.

Robert Edward Lee was born into a family that had fought courageously for American independence. His father, Henry Lee, known widely as Light-Horse Harry, had been a lieutenant colonel under General George Washington in the American Revolution. Robert's father had also been governor of Virginia and a member of the United States Congress. Robert's mother, Anne Carter Lee, came from a distinguished Virginia family.

It was with this background of privilege and distinction that Robert was born on January 19, 1807. His first home was the Lee estate, called Stratford. It was a beautiful plantation on the Potomac River in Westmoreland County, Virginia.

Robert was close to his mother, but never really knew his father very well. Henry Lee died when Robert was eleven. But Mrs. Lee made sure that her husband's admirable achievements were well known by her children. Robert was proud that his father had been a hero of the Revolution, a dedicated patriot, and a close friend of the nation's first President. The boy wanted to live up to that glorious image.

When Robert was still a young child, the family moved to the city of Alexandria, Virginia. The Lees were sorry to leave Stratford, but they also looked forward to living in Alexandria. The city was an exciting place, with docks where many foreign ships came and went, many shops, and so many interesting things to see and do.

Robert also spent a great deal of his childhood at Shirley, the plantation belonging to his mother's family. It was a splendid place, with twenty-five thousand acres of land filled with gardens, forests, fields, and stables. Mrs. Lee's family even had their own schools for the education of their children.

Robert's sisters, Ann and Mildred, attended the girls' school at Shirley. Robert and his brothers, Carter and Smith, went to the boys' school. It was at Eastern View, the home of one of their aunts. Right from the start, Robert was a serious student who excelled in all of his studies. He was also a fine athlete, and he especially loved to ride horses and swim.

As a teen-ager, Robert attended the Alexandria Academy, a fine local boys' school. Then, in July 1825, at the age of eighteen, he entered the United States Military Academy at West Point. West Point was a most demanding school. Cadets had to be well disciplined, dedicated to duty and classwork, in top physical condition, and determined to succeed. Robert had all of these qualities.

Cadet Lee didn't mind the hours of drilling, the tough military regulations, and the pressures of the highly competitive atmosphere. He excelled in everything and graduated with distinction. He won honors in tactics and artillery, and was second in chemistry, geology, and moral philosophy. Cadet Lee also did very well in engineering. On graduation day he ranked high in his class and was stamped as a future military leader.

In 1831, Robert E. Lee married Mary Anna Randolph Custis. She was the great-granddaughter of Martha Washington. The Custis family was very wealthy and owned a huge plantation on the banks of the Potomac River, across from Washington, D.C. The property, called Arlington, is now the Arlington National Cemetery. The original manor house still stands. Robert and Mary enjoyed a long and happy marriage. They had seven children, three boys and four girls.

Lee supervised different army con-
struction projects until the Mexican War
began in 1846. Now a captain, he was sent to
San Antonio, Texas, to serve with Brigadier
General John E. Wool. Wool had only a
small number of engineers, but with Lee to
lead them, they built roads and gun
emplacements and planned the routes the
troops would follow.

Captain Lee earned high praise for his
reconnaissance and engineering skills. He
had a remarkable ability to move troops and
material with the least amount of wear and
tear. He also knew how to choose battle loca-
tions that gave the greatest advantage to his
side, while causing problems for the enemy.

Lee's talents were absolutely critical in fighting a successful campaign. For his service in the Mexican War, Lee was highly praised and promoted to brevet colonel. General Winfield Scott said that Lee was the most promising junior officer and the greatest military genius in America.

From 1848 to 1852, Lee served in various assignments for the Corps of Engineers. He was then named superintendent of the United States Military Academy at West Point. He remained at this post for three years and made a deep impression on a whole generation of army officers. A number of them would serve with him on the side of the Confederacy in the Civil War.

Colonel Lee's next assignment was at Fort Cooper, Texas, commanding a regiment of cavalry. In 1859, while home on furlough, he received an order from the War Department. John Brown, an abolitionist, had led a group of citizens against the United States arsenal at Harpers Ferry, Virginia. Lee was to put down the rebellion and arrest John Brown. He fulfilled this assignment quickly and efficiently. It was Lee's first contact with the simmering fury over slavery that would soon explode into a bloody, four-year war.

Unlike many of his fellow Southerners, Robert E. Lee did not approve of slavery. He also did not approve of secession. The southern states were threatening to secede, or withdraw, from the United States of America, rather than give up slavery. Lee felt this was wrong. He could not imagine himself fighting against the United States. If secession came, he planned to return home and fight only in defense of his beloved Virginia.

In 1861, when the Civil War began, Robert E. Lee was asked to command the Union Army. He declined, then resigned his commission in the United States Army and took command of the military forces of Virginia. In May 1861, he was made a general in the Regular Confederate States Army. Lee accepted the responsibility because he felt it was his duty as a Virginian.

Many Southerners were convinced the war would be short and that they would win it. General Lee knew better. The North had more troops and more equipment. The North also had factories, raw materials, a large labor force, and good transportation and communications. The South had brave soldiers and determination, but could not otherwise match the North.

Under Lee's command, and with a major contribution from General Stonewall Jackson, the South won a series of major battles early in the struggle. These included the Seven Days Battle to protect the Confederate capital of Richmond, Virginia, and the Second Battle of Bull Run. There were other Confederate victories, but by 1863, the tide had turned against the South.

In midsummer of 1863, the Union forces, led by General George Meade, fought a three-day engagement against Confederate troops at Gettysburg, Pennsylvania. Lee's army was soundly defeated. It was the beginning of the end for the Confederacy.

Ragged and hungry, the South continued to fight until Richmond fell in the spring of 1865. The war finally ended on April 9, 1865, at Appomattox Court House, Virginia. On that day, General Lee handed over his sword to General Ulysses S. Grant, commander of the northern forces.

After the war, Lee had many opportunities to earn great wealth. Instead, he chose to become president of Washington College, a small school in Lexington, Virginia. It was later renamed Washington and Lee University, in his honor. As a college president he dedicated his last years to the education of young men from all parts of the South.

On October 12, 1870, Robert E. Lee died. He was buried on the grounds of the college he loved so well. His passing was mourned by Americans in every corner of the nation.